LET'S PLAY SPORTS!

TENNIS

by Tessa Kenan

TABLE OF CONTENTS

tadpole books

WORDS TO KNOW

ball

court

hit

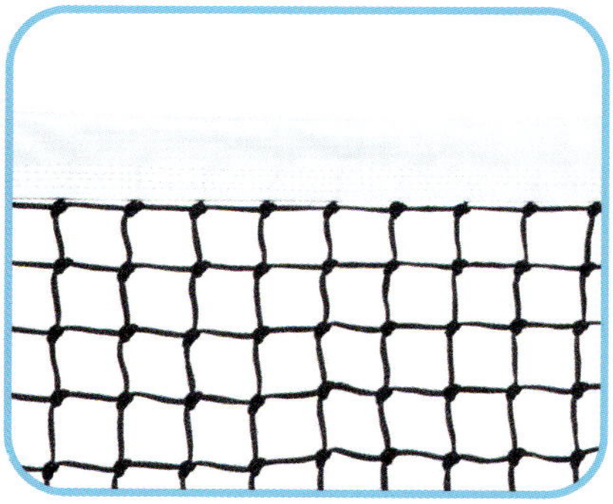

net

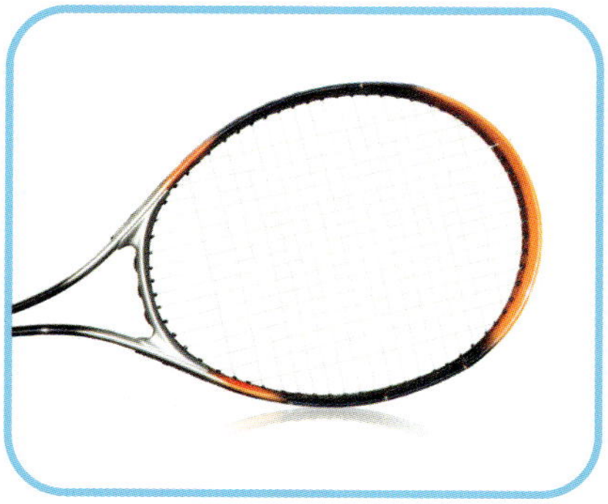

racket

serves

LET'S PLAY!

Let's play tennis!

We play on a court.

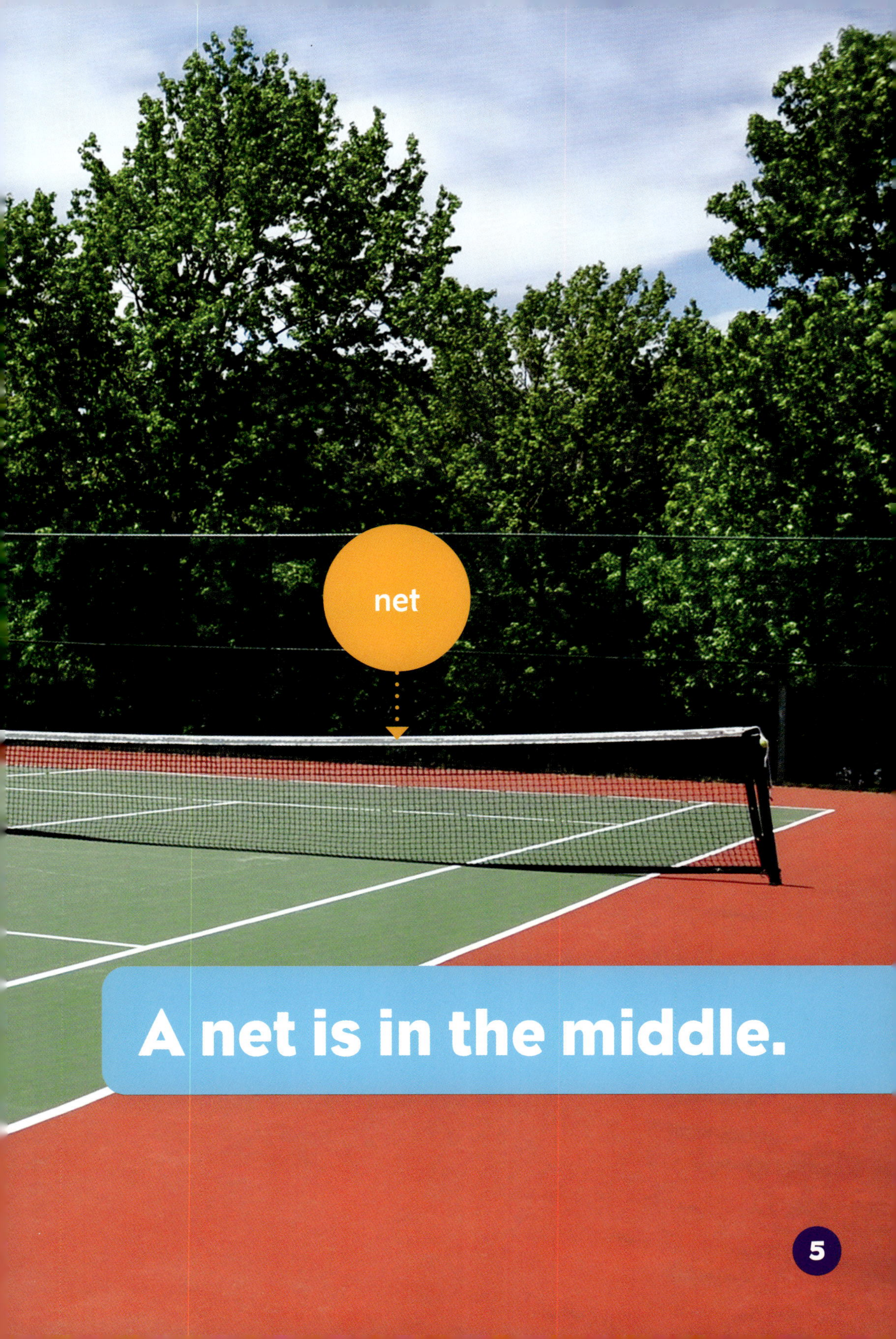

A net is in the middle.

The ball is yellow.

We hit it with a racket.

She serves the ball.

The ball flies over the net.

He hits the ball back.

Tennis is fun!

Do you want to play?

LET'S REVIEW!

What is this tennis player doing?

INDEX